2K to 10K:

Writing Faster, Writing Better, and Writing More of What You Love

Rachel Aaron

ISBN: 1548271101
ISBN-13: 978-1548271107

What's This Book About?

Once upon a time in the long ago summer of 2011, I wrote a blog post called "**How I Went from Writing 2,000 Words A Day to 10,000 Words a Day**" cataloging how I went from writing 2000 words during my daily writing sessions to averaging over 10,000 words a day without increasing the hours I spent writing. At the time, I was just excited to share what I'd learned about writing more efficiently with others (seriously, I felt like I'd discovered the cure to cancer and THE PEOPLE MUST KNOW!). Other than my excitement about sharing something cool, though, I didn't think much would come of it. But the Internet has a funny habit of proving me wrong, and a month after I put the post up, it went viral, spreading to more corners of the web than I'd known existed.

By the end of the year, my little how-to writing post had gotten so popular that I'm pretty sure more people knew me as "that 2k to 10k lady" than for my actual published books. And as the post continued to spread—popping up on the blogs of best selling authors, grad students, writing efficiency experts, and engineers working on cognitive learning AI system (how cool is that?!)—so did the requests for more. People from all over the world started writing me and leaving comments, asking questions like: How do you plot your novels? How do you figure out characters? How do you edit?

I answered many of these queries on my blog, but as I started building a body of "How I Write" posts, I realized that blogging wasn't actually the best medium for what I was trying to do. The multiple posts were confusing for new readers, and since I was answering questions as they came in rather than in logical order, there was no way for someone wanting to actually follow my process to know what came first. If only there was some way to put things in line, I thought to myself. A collection of writing advice arranged so that people who wanted to jump ahead to one part of the process could do so easily while others could start from the beginning. It was around this time that my friend (and hilariously funny writer) John Hartness sent me an e-mail asking why didn't I write a book? And once I finished pounding my head on my desk for not thinking of that myself, I did.

This book, **2k to 10k**, is designed to be a practical guide to writing efficiently based on the experience of a working author who doesn't eat if she doesn't produce good novels on a regular basis. The techniques I discuss are not limited to genre fiction: they can and have been used successfully by all sorts of authors writing everything from lyrical prose to technical nonfiction. The goal of this book is not to teach you how to write (there are lots of better books for that by far more venerated authors than myself), but how to get down what you're already writing *faster* and, hopefully, easier and with better end results.

The chapters that follow are a mix of the above mentioned blog posts (now reworked, updated, and re-edited) as well as several new sections on things like character development and novel structure that I wrote just for this e-book edition. So whether you're looking to speed through your tenth novel or trying to finish your first, I hope my tips and processes will help you reach and exceed your writing goals. Thank you and enjoy!

Rachel Aaron

How To Use This Book for Maximum Efficiency

This book comes in two parts. The first lays out my actual daily process for achieving enormous word counts with examples while the second outlines how I do all the background work that makes those word counts possible. Both parts are important to how I write quickly, but while I firmly believe the process laid out in **"How I Went from Writing 2,000 Words a Day to 10,000 Words a Day"** can help any writer double their daily words whatever their writing style, the methods outlined in part two—plotting, characters, and so forth—are more subjective.

I am a plotter, through and through. I thrive on lists, systems, and knowledge, and my methods reflect this. I am also impatient. I hate waiting, wasted time or effort, and I'll admit I have a bit of an obsession with efficiency. But while the systems I've laid out in part two of this book work amazingly for me, you are not me. You are your own writer, which means only you can understand how to best tell your stories. So, with that in mind, please don't think of anything in this book as gospel. There is no One True Way in writing. I'm only telling you what I discovered works for me in the hope that it might also work for you. Never be afraid to kick one of my steps to the curb if it doesn't help your process.

Still with me? Okay! Let's get writing.

Part I

How I Went from Writing 2,000 Words a Day to 10,000 Words a Day

When I started writing *The Spirit War* (*The Legend of Eli Monpress* novel #4), I had a bit of a problem. I'd just had a baby, and my life (like every new mother's life) was constantly on the verge of shambles. I paid for a sitter four times a week so I could get some writing time, and I guarded those hours like a mama bear guards her cubs—with ferocity and hiker-mauling violence. To keep my schedule and meet my deadlines, I needed to write 4000 (4k) words during each of these carefully arranged sessions. I thought this would be simple. After all, before I quit my job to write full time, I'd been writing 2k a day in the three hours before work. Surely with 6 hours of baby-free writing time, 4k a day would be nothing....

But (of course), things didn't work out like that. Every writing day, I'd sit down to add 4000 words to my new manuscript. I was determined, I was experienced, I knew my world. There was no reason I couldn't get 4k. But every night when I hauled myself away from the keyboard, my word count had only increased by 2k, the same number of words I'd been getting before I quit my day job.

Needless to say, I felt like a failure. Here I was, a professional novelist with three books about to come out, and I couldn't even beat the writing I'd done before I went pro. At first I made excuses, this novel was the most complicated of all the Eli books I'd written, I was tired because my son thinks four a.m. is an awesome time to play, etc., etc. But the truth was there was no excuse. I had to find a way to jack up my word count, and with months of 2k a day dragging me down, I had to do it *fast*. So I got scientific. I gathered data and tried experiments and ultimately ended up boosting my word count to heights far beyond what I'd thought was possible without increasing the time I spent writing each day, and all while making my writing better than ever before.

When I told people at ConCarolinas that I'd gone from writing 2k to 10k per day, I got a huge response. Everyone wanted to know how I'd done it, and I finally got so sick of telling the same story over and over again that I decided to write it down. So, once and for all, here's the story of how I went from writing 500 words an hour to over 1500, and (hopefully) how you can, too.

Quick note: *There are many fine, successful writers out there who equate writing quickly with being a hack. I firmly disagree. My methods remove the dross, the time spent tooling around lost in your daily writing, not the time spent making plot decisions or word choices. This is not a choice between ruminating on art or churning out novels for gross commercialism (though I happen to like commercial novels). It's about not wasting your time for whatever sort of novels you want to write.*

Drastically increasing your words per day is actually pretty easy. All it takes is a shift in perspective and the ability to be honest with yourself (which is the hardest part). Because I'm a giant nerd, I ended up creating a metric, a triangle with three core requirements: **Knowledge**, **Time**, and **Enthusiasm**. Any one of these can noticeably boost your daily output, but all three together can turn you into a word machine.

Side 1: Knowledge, or Know What You're Writing Before You Write It

The first big boost to my daily word count happened almost by accident. Used to be I would just pop open my laptop and start writing. I wasn't a total make-it-up-as-you-go writer—I had a general plot outline—but my scene notes were things like "Miranda and Banage argue" or "Eli steals the king."

This was how I had always written, but one day I got mired in a real mess. I'd spent three days knee-deep in the same horrible scene. I was drastically behind on my word count and I was facing the real possibility of missing my deadline... again.

It was the perfect storm of all my insecurities. The thought of letting people down mixed with the fear that I really didn't know what I was doing—that I wasn't a real writer at all, just an amateur pretending to be one. But just as I was working myself into a serious meltdown, I looked at my novel and suddenly realized that I was being an absolute idiot. Here I was, desperate for time, floundering in a scene, and yet I was doing the hardest work of writing (figuring out what needs to happen to move the story forward in the most dramatic and exciting fashion) in the most time-consuming way

12

possible (ie., in the middle of the writing itself).

As soon as I realized this, I stopped. I closed my laptop and grabbed my writing notebook. Then, instead of trying to write the scene in the novel as I had been, I started scribbling a very short, truncated version of the scene on paper. I didn't describe anything, I didn't do transitions or dialog. I wasn't *writing*, I was simply noting down what I would write when the time came.

It took me about five minutes and three pages of notebook paper to untangle my seemingly unfixable scene, the one that had just eaten three days of my life before I tried this new approach. Better still, after I'd worked everything out in shorthand, I was able to dive back into the scene and finish it in record time. The words flew onto the screen, and at the end of that session I'd written 3k words rather than my usual 2k, most of them in the last hour and a half.

Looking back, the solution was so simple I feel like an idiot for not thinking of it sooner. If you want to write faster, the first step is to know what you're writing before you write it. I'm not even talking about macro plot stuff— I mean working out the back and forth exchanges of an argument between characters, blocking out fights, jotting down fast descriptions. Writing this stuff out in words you actually want other people to read, especially if you're making things up as you go, takes FOREVER. It's horribly inefficient, and when you write yourself into a dead end, you end up trashing hundreds, sometimes thousands of words to get out. But jotting it down on a note pad? Takes no time at all.

If the scene you're sketching out starts to go the wrong way, you see it immediately, and all you have to do is cross out the parts that went sour and jump back to the good stuff. That's it. No words lost: no time wasted. It was god damn beautiful.

Those five minutes completely changed the way I wrote. Every writing session after this realization, I dedicated five minutes (sometimes more, never less) and wrote out a quick description of what I was going to write that day. Sometimes it wasn't even a paragraph, just a list of this happens, then that, then that. This one simple change—those five stupid minutes—boosted my word count more than any other single thing I've ever done. I went from writing 2k a day to 5k a day within a week without increasing my 6-hour writing block. Some days, I even finished early.

Of the three sides of the triangle, I consider knowledge to be the most important. This step alone more than doubled my word count. If you only try one thing out of this entire book, this is the one I recommend.

Side 2: Time

Now that I'd had such a huge boost from one minor change, I started to wonder what else I could do to jack my numbers up even higher. But as I started looked for other things I could tweak, I quickly realized that I knew embarrassingly little about how I actually wrote my novels. I'd kept no records of my progress. I couldn't even tell you how long it took me to write any of my last three novels beyond broad guesstimations, celebratory blog posts, and vague memories of past word counts.

It was like I started every book by throwing myself at the keyboard and praying for a novel to shoot out of my fingers before the deadline. And keep in mind this is my business. Can you imagine a bakery or a freelance designer working this way? Never tracking hours or keeping a record of how long it took them to actually produce the thing they were selling? Yeah, pretty stupid way to work.

If I was going to get serious about boosting my output, I had to know what I was outputting in the first place. So, I started keeping records. Every day I sat down to write, I would note the time I started, the time I stopped, how many words I wrote, and where I was writing on a spreadsheet (to see an example, check out the bonus section at the end of this chapter). I did this for two months, and then I sat down with my data to look for patterns.

Several things were immediately clear. First and most obvious was that my productivity was at its highest when I was in a place other than my home. That is to say, a place without Internet. The afternoons I wrote at the coffee shop with no wireless were twice as productive as the mornings I wrote at home.

I also saw that, while butt-in-chair time is the root of all writing, not all butt-in-chair time is equal. For example, those days where I only got one hour to write, I never managed more than 500 words in that hour. By contrast, on the days when I got five hours of solid writing time, I was clearing close to 1500 words an hour.

The numbers were clear. The longer I wrote, the faster I wrote, and, I believe, the better I wrote. This corresponding rise of word count and writing hours only worked up to a point, though. There was a definite words per hour drop-off around hour seven, when I was simply too brain-fried to go on.

But these numbers are very personal. The point I'm trying to make is that by recording my progress every day, I had the data I needed to start optimizing my daily writing. Once I had my numbers in hand, I rearranged my schedule to make sure my writing sessions were always in the afternoon—my most prolific time, according to my sheet, which was a real discovery! I would have bet money I was better in the morning—always at my coffee shop with no Internet, and always at least four hours long.

Once I set my time, I guarded it viciously, and lo and behold, my words per day shot up again. I was now up to an average of 6k-7k per writing day, all without adding any extra work hours. All I had to do was discover what made good writing time for me and then make sure the good writing times were the ones I fought hardest to get.

Even if you don't have the luxury of four uninterrupted hours at your prime time of day, I highly suggest measuring your writing during the times you do have to write. Even if you only have one free hour a day, trying that hour in the morning some days and the evening on others and tracking the results can make sure you aren't wasting your precious writing time on avoidable inefficiencies. Time really does matter.

Side 3: Enthusiasm

By this point I was flying high on my new discoveries. Over the course of three months, I'd boosted my daily writing from 2k per day to over 7k with just a few simple changes, and I was now actually running ahead of schedule for the first time in my writing career. But I wasn't done yet. I was absolutely determined to break 10k words a day.

I'd actually reached it before. Using Knowledge and Time, I'd already managed a few 10k+ days, including one where I wrote 12,689 words—two chapters—in seven hours. To be fair, though, I'd gotten that number while writing outside of my usual writing window, so it wasn't a total words-per-hour efficiency jump.

But that's the great thing about going fast. The novel starts to eat you, and you find yourself writing any time you can just for the pure joy of it. Even better, on the days when I broke 10k, I was also pulling fantastic words-per-hour, topping out at 1600-2000 words-per-hour, as opposed to my usual peak of 1500.

It was clear that these days were special, but I didn't know why. I did know that I wanted these days to become the norm rather than the exception, so I went back to my records (which I now kept meticulously) to find out what made the 10k days different.

As with everything else I'd discovered, the answer was head-slappingly obvious. The days when I broke 10k were the days when I was writing scenes I'd been dying to write since I planned the book. They were the candy bar scenes, the ones I wrote all that other stuff to get to. By contrast, my slow days (days when I was struggling to break 5k) corresponded to the scenes I wasn't that crazy about.

This was a duh moment for me, but it also brought up a troubling new problem. If I had scenes that were so boring I didn't want to write them, then there was no way anyone would want to read them. This was my novel, after all. If I didn't love it, no one would.

Fortunately, the solution turned out to be, yet again, stupidly simple. Every day, while I was writing out my description of what I was going to write for the knowledge component of the triangle, I would play the scene through in my mind and try to get excited about it. I'd look for all the cool little hooks, the parts that interested me most, and focus on those since they were obviously what made the scene cool. If I couldn't find anything to get excited over, then I would change the scene, or get rid of it entirely. I decided then and there that, no matter how useful a scene might be for my plot, boring scenes had no place in my novels.

This discovery turned out to be a fantastic one for my writing. I trashed and rewrote several otherwise perfectly good scenes, and the effect on the novel was amazing. Plus, my daily word count numbers shot up again because I was always excited about my work. Double bonus!

Life on 10k a Day

With all three sides of my triangle now in place, I was routinely pulling 10k words per day by the time I finished *Spirits' End*, the fifth and final Eli Monpress novel. I was almost two months ahead of schedule, and the novel had only taken me three months to write rather than the seven months I'd burned on *The Spirit War* (facts I now knew thanks to my records).

I had plenty of time to do revisions before I needed to hand the novel in to my editor, and I was more satisfied with my writing than ever before. There were several days toward the end when I'd close my laptop and stumble out of the coffee shop feeling almost drunk on writing. I felt as if I was on top of the world, utterly invincible and happier than I've ever been. Writing that much that quickly was like taking some kind of weird success opiate, and I was thoroughly addicted. Once you've hit 10k a day for a week straight, anything less feels like your story is crawling.

Now, again, 10k a day was my high point as a professional author whose child was now in daycare. At that point, I was writing 6-7 hours a day, usually 2 hours in the morning and 4-5 hours in the afternoon, five days a week. Honestly, I don't see how anyone other than a full-time novelist could devote this kind of time to writing, but that doesn't mean you have to be a pro to drastically increase your daily word count.

Of the people who've tried my triangle and gotten back to me (writers ranging from big professional authors to new writers working on their first novels), almost everyone has reported that they've doubled word counts. This means some have gone from 1k to 2k per session, while others have managed a lot more. Writing a very personal journey, but that doesn't mean it has to be a slow one. Sometimes, all it takes is a new way of looking at the problem to change everything.

Some of my success with increasing my word count is undoubtedly a product of experience as I also hit my million-word mark somewhere in the fifth Eli novel. Even so, I believe most of the big leaps in efficiency came from changing the way I approached my writing. Just like changing your lifestyle can help you lose a hundred pounds, changing the way you sit down to write can boost your words-per-hour in astonishing ways.

In the end, what matters most is that you're happy with your own writing, because—contrary to the myth of the tortured artist—a happy writer will always produce more and better than an unhappy one. And if you're still skeptical, I suggest you try my system for a week and track your numbers. You might surprise yourself.

BONUS! How I Wrote a Novel in 12 Days

The original blog post that spawned the chapter above was written directly after I finished *Spirit's End*, the fifth and final Eli Monpress novel. But though I firmly believed in everything I said, I was still nervous. At that point, every time I got on the subject of writing fast, I'd had to add the caveat that these magnificent numbers were achieved on the final two books of a five-book series, with my greatest progress showing up in the final half of the fifth novel. Even before I figured out how to speed up my writing, the end of a book has always gone faster than the beginning or the middle. It stands to reason, then, that the end of a series would be doubly so thanks to the momentum of the grand finale pulling me forward.

Because of these mitigating factors, it was hard for me to tell if my insane word counts were coming from my system or from the books themselves. Had I really turned myself into some sort of super writer, or was I just caught up in the end of a story I'd wanted to tell for years? Was Eli doing this, or was I?

So long as I was working on my Eli Monpress books, there was no way to tell. The real test would only come when I sat down to write a new book. If I could keep pulling crazy numbers with no familiar characters or well know world to prop me up, then I'd know for sure that my increased productivity came from me alone. So, after I turned in my edits on the final Eli book, I decided to put my theory to the test. I set out to write an entirely new story set in a completely new world as fast as I could.

A grand experiment, you could say. And this is how it turned out, taken straight from the writing worksheet I keep on my title page:

- Plotting started: July 17, 2011
- Plotting finished: July 20, 2011
- Novel started: July 21, 2011
- Novel ended: August 1, 2011

You're reading that right. I plotted the whole book, start to finish (as well as outlines for two sequels), in three days. And then I wrote the book in twelve. Actually, that's not even right. Check out my progress table on the next page, which I copied over from my writing progress spreadsheet:

Actual writing tracking table copied from the back of my Scrivener file:

Date	Time	Words	WPH	Loc.
	9:00 - 12:30	3680	1051	Home
7/21/2011	1:30 - 6:00	5125	1138	JJ's
	7:30 - 10:00	3877	1550	Home
7/22	1:30 - 6:30	6004	1200	JJ's
7/24 - 7/25	(edit for perspective switch, 3rd to 1st)			
	8:20 - 10:20	1925	962	Home
7/26	1:20 - 6:00	2194	487	JJ's
	9:00 - 10:00	1076	1076	Home
7/27	8:00 - 11:00	2527	842	Home
	1:00 - 6:00	7215	1443	JJ's
7/28	1:00 - 6:00	6372	1062	JJ's
7/29	8:30 - 11:30	3836	1278	Home
	12:30 - 6:00	7701	1400	JJ's
7/30	5:00 - 8:30	3373	963	JJ's
7/31	4:30 - 8:30	4509	1127	JJ's
8/1	8:00 - 11:30	4069	1627	Home
	1:00 - 6:20	7203	1359	JJ's

FINAL TOTAL: 62 hours, 73722 words, 1189 wph

What you're seeing here is the Time part of my writing triangle in action. As you can see from the numbers above, I actually wrote the book in nine days because I took the 23rd off and spent the 24th and 25th going back and switching the first three chapters from third person to first, which I count as editing, not writing. But even if we go ahead and count those, it still means that I wrote a novel—a *brand new* novel with a world and characters I'd never met before July 17th—in 12 days.

Sorry, Eli! It seems you can't claim the credit this time!

What I'd really like you to notice, though, are the numbers. The actual writing process only took me 62 hours. That's a week and a half at your standard 40-hour-a-week job. Not bad at all. Also, that 1189 final words per hour number is misleading. As I mentioned above, my words per hour are actually a curve with the first hour being the lowest, usually only about 500, reflecting the time it takes me to get settled into the writing mindset. After this, my words per hour generally go up with every hour spent writing, topping out at about 1500 when I'm in prime writing mode. This is the sweet spot, the place in writing where the story has you completely sucked in. I *live* for these hours.

Of course, this was just a first draft. By the time I was done editing, the book was closer to 95,000 words and had several new scenes. Full disclosure: I actually ended up editing this book more than any book I've ever written, but for reasons that had absolutely nothing to do with how fast I wrote the first draft. My problems came artistic choices I made in setting up the novel's non-standard structure. (I was trying to write a novel that had no villain, and it was a lot harder to pull off than I'd thought it would be). I firmly believe that I would have had to do the exact same amount of editing on this book whether I spent a week or a year on the initial draft. Fortunately, thanks to my new system, I didn't have to waste a year, and I actually went on to write another entire book in 2011 after this one was turned in.

So, Rachel, What Became of This 12-Day Book?

My agent sold it to Orbit Books! It's called *Fortune's Pawn,* and it's the first in an action-packed and romantic science fiction trilogy about a badass powered armor mercenary who gets herself into a lot of trouble, that came out in May of 2013 under my Rachel Bach pen name. (Not that I dislike being Rachel Aaron, but since this is science fiction and has a lot more sex, death, and cussing than my light hearted fantasy novels, Orbit wanted to differentiate my brands.)

Even now, years later, *Fortune's Pawn* is still one of my favorite things I've done, and the twelve days I spent writing it were some of the happiest and most exciting of my life.

I hope my process can help you write your own crazy, amazing, creative landslide of a novel. Even if you don't have the free time to get to 10k a day, doubling your daily word count still feels like flying. It's the most fun you can have on a page, guaranteed.

If Writing Feels Like Pulling Teeth, You're Doing It Wrong

As much fun as life can be on 10k a day, I'd like to pause here, before we get into the nitty-gritties of plot and so forth, and spend a moment with that most dreaded writing subject of all: *not writing.*

Oh yes, we've all been there. You sit down to get your daily words and end up reading Facebook for three hours instead. Or those nights when you promised yourself you'd write, but then someone calls and you get distracted and the next thing you know, it's midnight and you haven't typed a single word. Maybe your job is really stressful, and you just don't want to face plot problems, or maybe you don't even know why you're not writing. You just...aren't, and you can't seem to make yourself.

At times like this, the feeling of failure can be crippling. I used to lie in bed berating myself for hours. How could I say I wanted to be a writer when I wasn't even writing? It was all my fault. I was lazy; I was messing it up; I was failing my great dream—on and on and on.

It goes without saying that this kind of self-recrimination is harmful, but it's also a huge waste of time. I used to joke that if I spent half the hours I wasted feeling guilty about not writing on actual writing I'd have a whole shelf of novels. But even though I knew logically that I was being stupid, I couldn't seem to break the cycle, not even after I sold my series and quit work to write full time. Even when I had nothing else I needed to do except produce a novel, there would be whole weeks where I just couldn't seem to make myself sit down and write. And when I did force myself to put butt-in-chair and crank out some words, it felt like pulling teeth. Sometimes, the worst times, I wondered if I was even in the right profession, because while I loved *having written*, I didn't actually seem to like *writing*, and that terrified me.

But then, around the same time I got serious about writing faster, I suddenly realized that I'd been thinking about my writing in entirely the wrong way.

Paradigm Shove

At its core, writing is about entertainment. Good entertainment is interesting and engrossing at every stage. You're creating something you want others to enjoy, but if you aren't enjoying yourself while making it...Well, you can see the disconnect. So if you're finding every excuse under the sun not to write, that leaves two options: either you don't really want to be a writer (which is highly unlikely if you've gotten far enough into the process of authorship to be upset about not writing in the first place), or there's something wrong with your book.

Depressing as that statement sounds, this was actually an incredibly liberating discovery for me. I'd spent so long blaming my bad writing days on my own imagined lack of discipline, I'd completely ignored the fact that maybe the reason I didn't want to write was because I was *writing something I didn't like*. Maybe the characters were off or the tension was lacking. Hell, maybe the scene was just boring, and instead of forcing myself to keep trudging through it, I should be ripping it out.

This one little shift in thinking completely changed the way I approached my writing. Now, instead of treating bad writing days as random, unavoidable disasters to be weathered, like thunderstorms, I started treating them as red flags. It used to be, when I'd catch myself procrastinating, I'd launch into a diatribe of self blame that would leave me battered and more depressed than ever. Once I shifted my thinking, though, I stopped roughing myself up and started asking Why? Why don't you want to write? What's wrong? And while the answers were never pleasant (because really, it's no fun to realize you messed up and now you have to rewrite a scene, or a chapter, or half a book), they were progress, and they were necessary. They were also extremely good for me, because once I got my story back on the right track, my bad writing days vanished, my daily word counts shot up, the quality of my writing improved, and life in general got a whole lot better.

I always say that there is no one right way to write. Storytelling is a business of unique snowflakes. Every writer is different; every book is different; every reader is different. This is why it's so hard to give writing advice, because what works for me might be poison to someone else. But if I could make one absolute assertion, it would be this: **If you are not enjoying your writing, you're doing it wrong.**

A book is not a battle, nor is it a conquest. A book is a story, and telling it should be an enjoyable exercise. So the next time you don't want to write, don't waste time beating yourself up. Instead, stop and ask yourself *why*. Why do you not want to do this fundamentally enjoyable thing? What's really going on?

The answer might be terrifying, but here's a trade secret: the first step is the hardest. Admitting to yourself that there is a problem and you need to go back, rip out the words that aren't working, and rewrite is far and away the most painful part. Once you start actually writing again, especially when you start writing down the right path, the natural joy of the process returns and writing is fun again.

If your goal is to become a faster writer, the single most efficient change you can make isn't actually upping your daily word count, but eliminating the days where you are not writing. Also, you'll be a lot happier. Personally, I've found there is no greater sense of peace and contentment than that which comes from being happy with my stories. And as an extra bonus, your books will be better as well. Everyone wins!

So don't blame your subconscious when it doesn't want to write. Listen to it. Treat your instincts with respect, especially if they're telling you to stop. Let your daily writing be a joy instead of a chore, and everything else becomes easy.

Part II

Staying at 10k a Day: Tips for Efficient Plotting, Characters, Structure, and Editing

How I Plot a Novel in 5 Easy Steps

One of the most common questions in my email box is "How you do plot your novels?" Since this is clearly something people are curious about, I've put together a step-by-step process for how I go from "Hey, I should write a novel!" to "Let's get writing!" Some of these might seem a bit obsessive, but as I said back in part one of this book, the most important step of writing fast is knowing as what you're writing before you write it, and nothing helps that like lots of planning. As the great General Patton once said, "a pint of sweat saves a gallon of blood," and though bleeding on the page is part of writing, I like to keep my pain to the minimum necessary.

The Primordial Ooze of Storytelling

Planning a novel takes me anywhere from a few days to weeks, though it usually progresses in stages. Sometimes it starts with a great idea, one of those stop-in-your-tracks, can't-stop-thinking-about-it winners.

Other times it's several long simmering ideas suddenly coming together, or a character I always liked finally finding a home. However it happens, I start by writing things down. Nothing fancy, just jotting out ideas in a file that I keep in a folder labeled "Idea Bucket."

The vast majority of these half-baked ideas never become full novels. My computer is littered with the husks of cast-off stories. If you've wanted to be a novelist for any amount of time, chances are you have something similar: a notebook, an old story blog, even just a random collection of ideas in your head. This chaotic *mélange* of characters, settings, and story hooks may seem random and incomplete, but—excluding those rare and beautiful gems of novels that fall fully formed into your hands—the idea pool is a vital part of being a novelist. It is the primordial ooze from which all books emerge.

Deciding which of these newborn critters can withstand the process of actually becoming a book is the first and hardest step of plotting.

Step 0: Decide What Book to Write

When you sit down to write a book, you are embarking upon a very large project. As such, the first question you should be asking yourself isn't "Is this a good book?" but "Is this really the story I want to spend my time on?"

This can be a very tricky question, especially if you're really excited about one idea, like your main character, but you aren't yet sure what to do about the rest of the story. I can't give you a definitive test for which ideas are solid and which are duds, but here are some of the signs I look for to see if my current darling is ready to start the process of growing into a book:

1. I cannot stop thinking about it

You know how sometimes you get an idea that your brain will simply not shut up about? You think about it all the time, make up new stuff in the car instead of paying attention to where you're going, talk people's ears off about it, and get bouncing-up-and-down excited at the possibilities the story/world/character throws at you. These are marks of a really good idea that can carry you all the way to the end of a book.

2. It writes itself

This one goes part and partner with the can't-stop-thinking-about-it. I know a story is a keeper if I start writing scenes in my head without really trying. When you've got characters talking on their own or dramatic events unfolding right before your eyes, even if you're not sure how it all fits together yet, you've probably got a winner.

3. I can see the finished product

When I am super excited about a book, I can already see the finished product in my mind. I can see the sort of cover it would have, where it would sit in the bookstore, even the reviews. Most of this is wishful thinking (Why, Mr. Gaiman, I'm so delighted you liked my book!), but hey, I'm a fantasy author. Wishful thinking is my biz! What I'm really looking for here, though, is a feeling for the project as a cohesive whole. If you can look at your idea and already see roughly what it will be when you finish, even if you turn out to be completely wrong, that is a good sign that you've got the beginnings of something that can go the distance.

4. I can easily explain why other people would want to read it

This one is the trickiest and most subjective, but it's also the most commercial of the signs. When you try to sell a book to a publisher, an agent, or directly to the public, you're asking someone to spend their money (because time is money) on your idea. You're saying, "My book is worth reading," and if you're going to make that bold of a statement, you have to believe it yourself. You have to know *why* someone should care about your book. This can be as simple as "It's really fun!" or "My love story will be epic!" but it has to be there. If you can't easily explain to someone why your book is worth their time to read, then maybe you should reconsider whether this book is worth your time to write.

Can vs. Should

One of the hardest things I've had to learn as a writer is that while virtually any story *can* be a good book if done correctly, not every story *should*. It's possible to have an amazing idea and still lack the interest necessary to polish it to publication level shine. I can not tell you the number of books I've plotted, written 30k words in, and then abandoned because I simply could not stand to look at them another second. Every single one of these ideas looked great on paper, and maybe in another author's hands they could have been golden, but in the end I just didn't care enough to push through.

As someone who makes her living through writing, these stalled books are doubly disappointing. I'm pretty fast now at plotting and writing, but each of those stories still took time and work that I will never be paid for. It's like working a job for a month only to find out at the end that you're not getting a check. Even if you enjoyed yourself and everyone had the best intentions, you can't afford to work for free. That said, though, I don't regret abandoning the ideas that didn't work. No amount of money is worth forcing myself to write a story I don't like, especially since I couldn't sell such a loveless book anyway.

If I have any regrets about these failed books, it's that I didn't recognize my lack of interest sooner. That's what Step 0 is about. You don't need to have a plot or characters or even an ending at this point, but you do need a certainty that the idea floating in your head is something that will not only hold your interest not only through the time it takes to write, edit, and polish a manuscript, but will, once finished, do whatever it is you want this project to do (get you an agent, please your editor, sell fantastically, etc.). Even if you're not selling your stories yet, your writing time is precious, often gained at the expense of other worthwhile activities. Don't waste it on a book you don't love.

Step 1: Get Down What You Already Know

Now that I've decided this is the novel I want to write, the first thing I do is put down everything I already know about the book. These are usually the ideas that exploded into my mind and made me want to write the story in the first place. Sometimes it's a character or situation, sometimes it's a magical system or a setting. Whatever it is, I write it down quickly and efficiently. I don't bother with details and I don't force myself to write past the initial flash of interest. At this point I'm just locking down the rough ideas that excite me about the book.

I use this step to codify and organize what I already know about my world, characters, and plot, which is usually very little at this stage. But, by putting this very little down, I have laid a basic framework and can now see the holes I'll need to fill in before any actual writing can begin. You'll know this step is finished once you have to start making up new things in order to move forward. Depending on how much you already know about your world, plot, and characters, this step can be one of the shortest or one of the longest.

Scrivener Shout-Out

This is also the step where I make my Scrivener file. For those of you who haven't tried Scrivener yet, it is hands down the best writing program I've ever tried. It's basically a word processor that lets you jump around between chapters in real time via a list on the sidebar, make notes on the text, and organize all your world building/characters/notes in intuitive folders.

For example, I keep all my actual writing in the Manuscript section divided by chapter, and then, in the research section, I have folders for Setting, Characters, and Plot with a separate area for my cuts file (where I put big blocks of text that I've cut out of the story but can't bring myself to delete yet) and my writing worksheet, which is the table I use to keep track of my word counts. And when you're done writing, Scrivener will quickly and competently compile your book into any document or e-book format you can think of, including Kindle, ePub, MS Word docs, and PDFs.

You can see Scrivener in action with all its millions of features at www.literatureandlatte.com. And no, they didn't ask me or pay me to say any of this. I am getting no kickbacks. I just REALLY freaking like Scrivener (I'm actually writing this in Scrivener right now.) You don't need it to write, of course—I wrote 5 books without it—but I do recommend it as an excellent writing program.

Step 2: The Basics

Now that I've gotten down what I know already, it's time to start filling in the gaps. This is the part of the process where I figure out the bare bones of the three pillars of story: characters, plot, and setting. You know, that high school lit class stuff. As I just mentioned in my Scrivener love letter, I like to make folder for each of these so I can just throw anything remotely related under the appropriate header, but you don't have to do that. So long as you can keep your notes straight, any system from complex writing diagrams to paper napkins will do.

Now, what bare bones am I talking about? Here's my list:

For **Characters**, I need: The Main Characters (usually 2-4), the Antagonists (1-2), and the Power Players (as many as needed). The numbers are very subjective and change from book to book, but you get the idea. MCs and Antagonists are self-explanatory, but Power Players are the people in the story who are not primary characters but are nevertheless very important to the setting. Think Etmon Banage in my Eli Monpress books or Dumbledore in Harry Potter. You know, the BIG names who move and shake in the world.

I'm not doing detailed character sheets yet. I'm just getting down the basics: names, motivations, and the general sense I have of them as a character. Physical descriptions and histories come later. All I care about right now is how this person relates to the story. I've had character sheets that were nothing but a name and a one-line description at this stage of things, and that's perfectly fine.

For **Plot**, I need: The end and the beginning, in that order. Figuring out the end of a book is my number one priority. After I've got my start point and my end point, I fill in whatever twists/scenes/climaxes I've already thought up. I don't worry about how these scenes link together yet, or even if the events are in the right order. I'm just getting down the general thrust of things.

This is also the point where I determine if this book is a stand-alone novel or part of a series. If it's a stand-alone, I have to be sure my ending will resolve everything. If it's going to be a series, then I work out the end of the larger meta plot and where this current book's plot fits into the larger scheme.

This kind of super long planning might sound like overkill, but you really want to nail this sort of thing down early. There is nothing worse than getting to the end of your stand-alone novel only to discover it's actually the first book in a series you've done no planning for. If you don't think you can wrap up all your story threads neatly in one novel, either cut some characters, or go ahead and think of this book as the first in a series. Trust me—deciding on this now saves a lot of work and heartache further down the line.

Finally, this is the point where I figure out what

kind of story I want to tell. An adventure can have a love plot, and a love story can be an adventure, but the tone and drama of a romance is completely different from a thriller. It's important that I decide which story is going to be the primary tale as soon as possible. Otherwise I risk ending up with a story whose voice doesn't match its meat, which is just about the worst problem ever to try and fix in an edit. Nothing is more pervasive in a novel than tone, so if you don't want to risk a complete rewrite down the line (I have done this, and it SUCKS), do yourself a favor and nail your voice down early. (Writing a few throwaway practice scenes can really help with this step, especially if you're also debating on whether to write the book in first person or third.)

For **Setting**, I need: the magical system (if there is one), the basic political system, and the general feel of the places where the action will be happening. What is the technology level of this world? What kind of culture are we in? Who has power and why? How did the world get to its current state? If I'm writing a fantasy, I'll also do a creation story and work out the pantheon at this point. For science fiction, I figure out how humans got into space. So on and so forth.

This step changes wildly from book to book. I basically just write until I feel I've got a firm hold on what kind of world the action takes place in (though, again, I don't sweat the details yet). What we're doing here is the purest form of world-building, and it should be enormously fun. If you are not having fun putting your world, characters, and plot together, you need to go back to Step 0 and seriously reconsider if this is the book you should be writing.

Step 3: Filling In The Holes

By the time I move on to step 3, I have a solid feel for the basics of my story. I know how my novel starts and ends plus a few big scenes. I know who's in it and where it's taking place. Now comes the nitty-gritty of making everything work together.

When I reach this step, I like to fill in the plot first because the plot is what ties everything together. Thanks to the work I've already done, I know the story's beginning, so that's where I start. I go to the beginning, look at my world and my characters' motivations, and ask "What happens next?" Once I've got that down, I ask again, building the plot step by step until I get stuck.

I *always* get stuck. Fortunately, it's no big deal. Whenever I don't know what happens next, I just jump further down the line, either straight to the ending (which I already worked out, clever me!) or to one of the big scenes I was excited about back in step 2. When I get there, I look at my world and my characters and ask "How did this happen?" And then I work backwards from there until I either reach the place where I got stuck the first time or I get stuck again. If that happens, I just jump to another point and pick up from there until all the dots are connected.

Sometimes though, I get *really* stuck. Like, I

have no idea how two scenes are connected, or I realize my ending comes out of nowhere and I have absolutely no clue how to make it fit neatly. When this happens, it's very tempting to think your whole plot is borked, but here's a trade secret: there's no such thing as an unfixable plot. Often, you don't even have to figure out a clever solution, you just need to discover *why* something isn't working and the solution will simply appear.

One of the earliest lessons I learned about writing was that if I was stuck, it was because I didn't know something. Just as we discovered back in the 2k to 10k section, knowledge is the grease that makes books go. When a plot won't move forward, it's almost always because there's something I don't know about the characters or the world or why this event is actually happening. Once I figure it out, I can unstick even the most stubborn plot. So, when I get really, seriously stuck, I let the plot go and start working out other things.

This is where I work out the detailed history of my world and spend time with my characters to figure out how they got to this point and what they're thinking. And if that still isn't enough to get me moving again, I set down in ludicrous detail what's going on in the world at the moment the plot is stuck. I especially map out exactly what the villains are doing. This alone is often enough to snap the plot back into place, or—even better—come up with a new plot point that works a hundred times better than the old one. But whether you're fixing a broken plot point or creating a new one, knowledge is the key. Don't beat your head against what isn't working; just focus on discovering *why*. Once you've got that, everything else will shake itself out in short order.

Learn from My Fail

I know I just said that knowledge can get stuck plots moving again, but there is such a thing as knowing too much. Many years ago, I was working on a sweeping epic fantasy. I was a young author, eager to do things right, and I'd read online that a writer should know her world inside and out. With this in mind, I set to work Building My World (TM). I wrote and wrote and wrote for days, churning out all this absurdly detailed world-building information that had nothing to do with my story. Things like the political backdrop of wars that happened five hundred years before the plot and proper table manners in countries across the sea that I was never going to visit. And then, about halfway through naming the different dead princes of the empire that had fallen a thousand years ago, I threw the novel away in disgust.

I'm not saying this will happen to you. If you enjoy planning out your worlds to that level of detail, go for it, but remember that everything can be taken too far. You can absolutely make yourself sick of your world before you've even started writing, if you're not careful.

Step 4: Building a Firm Foundation

I know I've reached the end of step 3 when I can write out my whole plot, start to finish, with no blanks or skipped scenes. By this point, I've usually gotten stuck enough to have detailed sheets for all my characters and notes for all my major settings. I also have a solid voice in my head for the book and I know what POV I'm using (first, third, swapping chapters between characters, etc.). Finally—and this is where things get a little hokey—I know I'm ready to move on to the next part of my planning when the feel of the book becomes tangible.

I've never bought into muses or any of the more spiritual parts of writing, but I will admit that all my books have a unique feel, almost like a taste in my mind that belongs to that book alone. I can't say exactly what causes a novel to gel into this nebulous presence, but I never move on to the next step until I can taste the book clearly. Once I've got it, it's time for step 4.

This is actually a new step for me. Back in the old days I would dive into a novel as soon as I had a plot and my feel. Now that I'm writing faster, though, I've discovered that taking a day to do one extra step of refinement can save weeks of trouble down the line. If the basics (the plot, characters, and settings we laid out back in Step 3) are the scaffolding, this is the concrete foundation that will support my novel through the writing and edits to come.

At this point, I always:

Make a time line. I didn't have time lines for the first 4 Eli novels and OMG did it bite me in the ass. Lesson finally learned, I now make time lines not just for the events of the novel itself, but the important bits of history before it as well. I especially make sure to note the relative ages of all my characters and how long everyone's known everyone else. Yes, it's annoying and nitpicky, but time lines have saved my bacon many, many times over now, and I very, very much recommend making one. Trust me, you are not nearly as good at keeping track of things in your head as you think you are.

Draw a map. Actually, I usually end up doing this back in step 2, but if I don't have a map by now I'll make one, usually several, of the world at large as well as all my important locations. I also write out short descriptions of each place. This helps me describe locations consistently and removes the burden of making this shit up as I go along.

Write out who knows what, when. This is usually just a quick list where I look over my plot and jot down the flow of important information to make sure I haven't done something dumb like have the protagonists making a decision using information they wouldn't actually know yet. I use this list less as a resource and more as a final double check on my plot.

Make sure I **memorize everyone's particulars**. I

need to know name spellings, physical descriptions, and ages for all my major cast members by heart. Can't have anyone's name dropping vowels or eyes changing color mid-story, can we? I also make sure to memorize important places, relative distances, organizations, and whatever else I need to avoid stupid mix-ups and bad assumptions while writing.

Write out a scene list. This one is a little odd. Here, I take that plot I wrote out at the end of step 3 and break the action down into scenes. Next, I group these scenes into chapters to make a nice little list. For example, the first chapter of *The Spirit Thief* would look like this:

Chapter 1
- Eli charms his way out of prison
- The king of Mellinor discovers Eli has escaped, is moved to safer quarters
- Eli and Josef take advantage of the confusion and kidnap the king.

My chapters usually consist of three scenes each, though I've done as few as two and as many as five before. It really depends on how long you like your chapters and what's going on in the book at the time. Chapter breaks should also increase dramatic tension, so I try to take that into account as well. If the end of a chapter is a good place to put down a book, that's exactly what the reader will do, so I make sure I never give them the chance. Putting my book down should be the hardest thing my reader has to do that day. Authorship is a merciless business!

Word count estimation. Once I have a rough idea of how many chapters I'll have from my scene list, it's time to do an even rougher estimation of how long this book is going to be. I know from personal experience that my chapters tend to run between 6k and 7k words, so if I multiply the number of chapters by that, I can approximate how long the finished draft will be. Of course, this number is a *very* rough estimate, but doing a check like this is not so much about accuracy as it is about having an early warning signal. If, for example, I've lined up all my scenes and found that I have 30 chapters worth of plot, then I know I will need to cut something to avoid ending up with an 200,000 word unpublishable monster (The sweet spot for traditional publishing is between 80k and 100k, though Fantasy can go up to 120k.)

It is a thousand times easier to cut scenes at this stage than to cut them after they're written. Even if you don't know your average chapter length yet, if you're doing more than one scene per chapter, chances are they won't be shorter than 4k. Counting your chapters and multiplying to get a rough idea of how big your book will be is a great way to avoid painful cutting further down the line.

Finally, I do a **boredom check**. A boredom check

is where I think through my plot, imagining the story in my head as thought it were a movie. There's no sound or dialog; I just go through the story, scene by scene, searching for slow spots, things that don't make sense, or anywhere that seems to lag. If I can't visualize something or I skip a scene, I stop and figure out why.

The point of this exercise is that when you cruise through your plot visually, you're looking your story as a reader instead of a writer. Your writer mind might consider a scene necessary for plot reasons, but if your reader mind is bored, it'll skip right over that scene to get back to the good stuff. This is a giant red flag. I don't want my readers to skip over anything I write, and I don't want to waste my time writing boring crap no matter how nicely it fits into the plot. Ripping a scene out of a finished plot can feel really scary, but this is all part of the "Be excited about everything you write" component of the 2k to 10k writing triangle. It's much better to stop and think up a new scene now, when rearranging the story is easy, than to try and wrestle with a dull scene further down the road.

Step 5: Start Writing!

At this point I'm usually chomping at the bit to get writing. I know my world, I know my characters, I know my voice, I know exactly what's going to happen and why, and I know the climax I'm working toward. I'm confident and ready, so much so that the scenes are usually writing themselves in my head already. All I have to do is sit down and let the words out. This is the mindset that gets 10k words a day.

Writing Is Not a Performance Art

No matter how carefully you've plotted, though, chances are the story will change dramatically as you write. Characters will mature and deepen, you'll discover plot holes you never considered, and ideas you thought were amazing will start looking played and stupid once you get into the thick of things. All of this is natural to the writing process, and part of being a successful plotter is knowing when to let go of your plans and just roll with things.

Just because you've already made a decision doesn't mean you can't make a better one. No one has all their good ideas at once, so don't be afraid to let go and just write. Plotting exists to make your life easier, not harder; to lift you up, not hold you back. No one is looking over your shoulder to see if you mess up, and even if you change everything mid course, you can always go back and set thing right in the edit. This is one of the great blessings of being a writer. Within your book, you are god, and nothing is final until you say so. Writing is not a performance art, so don't be afraid to let everything be a total broken mess for a while, if that's what it takes to get your story right.

Characters Who Write Their Own Stories

Back in the chapter on plotting, you probably noticed that I don't have a specific stage where I created my characters in detail. That wasn't an oversight. I like to let my characters grow up along with the world and the story as I put together my plot. This way, rather than creating an entire character out of whole cloth and then either trying to wedge them into the plot (frustrating) or building the plot around them (limiting and problematic), everything gets made together to create a unified whole that, coincidentally, often makes plotting way easier.

Now, of course, this is by no means the only way to work. Many great authors start everything with the characters and work from there, creating people and then throwing problems at them to see what they'll do. But if you're like me and like to keep control of your story (or if you, like me, have particularly loudmouthed, opinionated characters), such methods can be excessively frustrating. Letting your characters run your story can feel a lot like trying to herd a pack of rowdy cats through an increasingly difficult series of hoops. With this in mind, I find it much easier (and far less stressful) to think of myself less like a herder and more like a wagon driver with my characters as the horses. They're the ones out in front pulling the story forward, but I'm the one with the reins, and, together, we get where we're going.

Drivers vs. Passengers

Have you ever stopped, stepped back, and looked at what a character actually does for a story? As an example, take your favorite book. Now, remove the main character completely. What happens to the story? Does the world end because the hero wasn't there to save it? Do the bad guys win? Does anything happen at all?

Characters are more than actors. In a good story, they are the engines whose desires push the plot forward. It is the unicorn's determination to find out if she is truly the last that kicks off everything in Peter S. Beagle's *The Last Unicorn*. If she didn't care, if she never existed, Schmendrick would still be in Mommy Fortuna's circus, Molly would still be a cook, Haggard would go unchallenged, and the unicorns would remain in the sea forever. This is an example of how a character can completely drive the action of their story, even if the key events don't start with them.

On the other side of the coin, look at Harry Potter. Where the unicorn actively seeks her destiny,

Harry's is thrust upon him. He could have refused the call to go to Hogwarts all together and the events of the plot would still have dragged him in. He is a character who is acted *upon* (as most characters with a great destiny are). The story came and whisked him away, and Harry had very little say in the matter. But Harry didn't refuse to go to Hogwarts. Quite the opposite, he embraced his new wizarding life wholeheartedly. This is important, because though Harry's destiny as The Boy Who Lived meant he was in this tale like-it-or-not, his *choice* to jump into the wizarding world and become Harry Potter is where his story really begins.

A character's story comes from their choices. If Harry had rejected the call to go to Hogwarts and instead run off to join the circus as a snake charmer, that would have been his story, not his time at wizard school. This ability to make decisions that change the direction of the plot is called *character agency*, and it is vital. Even if characters start out as passengers in the story, like Harry did, they must eventually get up front and start pulling or they'll never be anything more than a point of view riding through their own book. Even if they're the Chosen One at the center of everything in the universe, a character who doesn't decide doesn't have a story, and they will never be anything but flat cardboard no one cares about.

Fair Enough, Rachel, But What Does Agency Have to Do with Writing Fast?

Because, if you do it right, characters with

proper agency will *write their own stories*. And they will do it faster, better, and more naturally than you ever could.

Remember when I talked about how I fill the parts of my plot that I don't know yet by asking "What comes next?" or "How did this happen?" Well, most of the time the answers to those questions come from my characters, and in a circular turn, these answers serve to develop the characters who give them. This is how plot and character development go hand in hand, and it can be confusing, so let me give you an example from my own experience.

Back when I was plotting *Spirit's End*, the fifth and final of my Eli Monpress novels, I ran into a thorny problem. I needed to get Eli, my charming wizard thief of a main character, away from his oppressive lady friend so that he could rejoin the rest of the cast for a reunion scene I knew I wanted near the middle of the book. Trouble was, I had no idea how I was going to get Eli away from Benehime (the aforementioned oppressive lady friend). She certainly wasn't going to just let him go, and I'd already used the fact that Eli couldn't escape on his own as a big plot point in the previous novel.

It was the characters themselves who came to my rescue. To answer the question "What happens next?" I put Eli and Benehime's motivations against each other. This sparked an enormous argument that ended up with Benehime actually kicking Eli out of her own volition. The resulting scene became a pivotal bit of character development for both of them as well as a great plot solution for me. Win all around!

The point I'm trying to make here is that when you let your characters make their own choices, they become real people who can tell you where they need to go. By making your character's decisions and needs part of your plot right from the beginning, treating them as active participants in the novel rather than passengers on a rollercoaster to the climax, you end up with easier plotting, faster writing, and better stories.

If I'd tried to get Eli away from Benehime and back with the other characters by myself, I would have had to pull some serious *deus ex machina* plot device magical portal malarkey to make it work. But because I respected my characters and trusted them to figure out their own lives, I didn't have to. The characters pulled themselves out of the hole. They wrote their own story, and that made all the difference.

Character Sheets

So let's get into the actual writing down of character details. Like most authors, I like to make a sheet for each major personality for easy organization and reference, but the sheets themselves are highly variable. If you look around online for character reference sheets, you'll find millions. Some are bogglingly enormous with hundreds of questions detailing histories and favorite colors and all sorts of minutiae I probably don't even know about myself. Others are simpler—just names, basic facts, maybe a line or two for history. I can't tell you which ones to use because I bounce all over. I've had characters with huge questionnaires full of information and characters who were little more than a few lines on notebook paper. Some characters just needed more than others. It really depends on the person and what I required from them at the time.

Sometimes my people will walk into my head fully formed; other times I can mess with a character for weeks before I understand why they do what they do. My process for character creation is as wildly varied as the characters I come up with, and while the control freak in me wishes I could streamline things a little, I doubt I'll ever create the One True Character Sheet. That said, however, every character I create starts like this:

Name:
Age:
Physical Description:
I like:
I hate:
More than anything, I want:

This is the stuff I fill out when I'm first getting a character down (this would be during step 2 of plotting for those of you keeping track). As you see, it's very basic, and almost all of it changes several times before actual writing begins. The first three fields are strictly for reference. (Unless you've created a world where hair color indicates status, no character was ever defined by the shade of his locks.) It's the last three are actually important, because these determine who the character is.

As Facebook has taught us, a person's likes and dislikes tell us way more about them than any biography could. I went a step further, adding an "I hate" section, and the two of these combined can tell you a lot about your character's personality. Are they a hard worker who likes getting stuff done and hates lazy people? Or are they a laid-back sort who likes good times with friends and resents being bossed around? Do they like having power over others, or do they hate bullies? Little stuff like that can reveal so much, even if you don't know why they're like that yet, but the most important question by far is: what does the character want?

Every character in a book, even the most minor, needs a motivation. They have to want something. This is where agency comes from, because characters who want things are the ones who push the story to get them. Wants can be simple and generic (fame, freedom, wealth, not dying, make this wolf stop eating me, etc.) or complex and setting specific (earn a one million gold bounty, master my magic, take my place as the true king, destroy the One Ring, etc.). In minor characters, simple motivations are good, but for your main cast, heroes and antagonists, motivation is also a plot decision. These are the people whose wants should be driving the book. Villains who want to take over the world are a classic example of character motivation and plot working together.

Once I've got these basics down for my most important people, the rest of the character (their history, love interests, destiny, potential roll in the end of the world, and so forth) develops right along with the plot and the setting as I finish up step 3 of plotting. This is partially because plot and character development should be so tightly intertwined they can't be separated and partially because coming up with deep, nuanced, well-rounded characters in a vacuum is *really freaking hard*. By letting your people grow up along with the world that created them and the events that will shape them, everything becomes easier and more believable, and (hopefully) nothing will need to be forced into place.

Doing things this way always reminds me of braiding. You're weaving all these events, places, and people together to make the rope of your story. Each bit is its own unique line that has a beginning and an end, but all of them get twisted together into the smooth whole of the novel. If you've done this bit right, then by the time you're ready to start writing you'll have a cast of agency-filled characters whose understandable and natural decisions drive your plot toward a thrilling and satisfying conclusion, with little to no meddling required from your end.

All you have to do is be there to write it down.

The Story Architect

One of the things I've always disliked about telling people I'm an author is the amount of cultural baggage that comes with the name. For many people, the word "writer" conjures up images of a temperamental genius drinking whiskey and having terrible love affairs in his (*always* his) low-rent tenement while waiting for the muse to strike. I hate this idea partially because it is inaccurate; most authors I know have families and (with a few notable exceptions) healthy relationships with alcohol. Mostly, though, I object to the tortured genius stereotype because of the incredible powerlessness it implies. I hate the idea that inspiration is something that comes to you rather than something you reach for, and I *really* hate the notion that you have to be some kind of born genius to write good book. I also abhor the belief that you have to be unhappy or emotionally compromised to make art. I am much more productive when I'm happy, sober, and stable.

In my experience, writing is an active undertaking, not a passive one. I don't sit around waiting for stories to come to me. I pursue them relentlessly, testing and building my ideas until they're strong enough to hold up not just one novel, but entire series. When I'm planning out character arcs and tying themes together through conscious story structure choices, I'm not a temperamental artist enslaved to the whims of her muse. I am a story architect building glittering cathedrals in the desert for all the world to marvel at.

On the surface, shifting my role as writer from whimsical artist to practical architect might seem limiting. After all, authors have almost endless freedom to create, while architects are constantly being dragged down by reality. They have to consider gravity, physics, the limits of their materials, and the whims of their clients. And yet, despite these barriers, architects throughout history have created amazing works of beauty that are still usable by people as houses, halls, and public spaces. But though it might seem that by identifying with the architect I am constraining the possibilities of what I can create, the truth is that writers are also tied down to reality, only our boundaries are much harder to calculate.

It's easy to claim that writing is an act of pure, free-wheeling imagination, but anyone who's ever sat down to actually tell a story knows that there are a few things you can't get around. Though technically there are no rules for how to write a book, certain methods definitely work better than others, and if you ever want to sell your stories commercially, your options are even narrower. But don't let that get you down. The truth is, unless your novel is *really* out there, chances are you're already following a common story structure without even knowing it.

However they come to be, whether you're a plotter or someone who lets their tale unfold organically, all stories have structure. But for those who learn to embrace and work with the rules rather than against them, well-executed story structure will let you create tension and plot twists like nothing else. Just as a really good architect can create a space that is both stunning artwork and functional building, so can a skilled story architect use reader expectation to craft masterful, thrilling, and complex books that seem effortless to the outside observer.

Sound like fun? Good. Let's begin.

Three-Act Structure, Now with More Fire

Almost all modern novels fall into the three-act structure. First, it's an incredibly good way to deliver a story. Second, it's the form almost all movies follow, and since movies are the dominant form of popular storytelling these days, it's the form you and your readers are probably most familiar with. Chances are you probably already think in a three-act structure and don't even realize it. I first encountered the idea as an English major over ten years ago, but even I didn't realize that I was unconsciously following the three-act structure until I was writing my fourth book. It's that pervasive. Fortunately, it's also that good.

So what is this magical structure? Well, there are many ways to describe it, but this is undoubtedly my favorite:

- ○ **Act I**, put your characters in a tree.
- ○ **Act II**, light the tree on fire.
- ○ **Act III**, get your characters out of the tree.

Act I is the introduction: here are our characters; here is the world; here is the beginning of our action. Everything is ticking along happily until *something happens* and the story begins. In lit major speak, this *something* is called the Inciting Action, but since this isn't a literature class, we're going to talk about Star Wars instead.

The original *Star Wars: A New Hope* is a classic example of the three-act structure in action. In Act I, we have Darth Vader capturing the rebels and Princess Leia sending her plea to Obi-Wan Kenobi, followed by a cut to Tatooine where young Luke is a just a farm boy dreaming of bigger things. This is our setup. We meet our major characters, we get a taste for the larger world and the problems it faces, and we see how the game board is set. Our characters have been placed in the tree, so to speak. We've also had some excitement with Leia's capture, so we are interested and engaged and ready to see what's going to happen next.

But though we've got all this action at the beginning, the story of Star Wars doesn't actually start until the death of Luke's aunt and uncle. This is the Inciting Action, the match that lights the tree on fire. Before this, our hero, Luke, was not engaged in the larger universe. He was just a moisture farmer boy who shot womprats on the weekends. But now, tragedy has set him on his journey. Act II has begun, and things are catching on fire left and right as the complications begin to pile up.

You might notice that much of the action in Star Wars happens in Act II. This is true universally. Act I is set up; Act II is action; Act III is resolution. It's the classic story mountain that you learn about in high school: rising action, climax, falling action, denouement. Act II is the run up to the climax. The fire is climbing up the tree, the characters are in danger, the stakes are rising— *what will happen*?! Act II is very exciting, tension-filled stuff, which is why it's normally the longest act. You want to spend the most time in the best part of the story. Lingering over setup in Act I can lead to a boring, flabby, slow start that can turn off readers. You want to get your characters into that tree as efficiently and interestingly as possible so you can move on to the fun part, i.e., lighting things on fire.

Act II ends when it's time for the climax. For *Star Wars*, this would be the assault on the Death Star. Act III is what the complications of Act II lead up to. It's the payoff, the big event. We're heroically getting those people out of that burning tree before it collapses and kills us all. This is where your characters put everything on the line, use the Force, defeat the bad guy, and save the world.

Because it comes at the end, Act III has a lot of tension. All the buildup from Act II boils over here, but so much excitement can lose its punch if you try to sustain it too long. Have you ever gone to an action movie where the final fights seemed to drag on forever? So much so that you actually started getting tired of explosions? This is the danger of trying to hold Act III's energy past its prime. We can only stay on the edge of our seats for so long before we start getting tired. But at the same time, Act III is your main event. You don't want to rush things, but you don't want to overstay your welcome either, and so you end up in a balancing act that even the biggest names have messed up.

Unfortunately, there is no failsafe plan for a perfect third act. There's no plan for a perfect first or second act either. That's why this is a structure and not a formula. Any author can put three-acts together, but you still have to be a good writer to pull them off to their best effect. That said, being aware of these structures and understanding their strengths and limitations can make the art of knowing how to keep your tension at that perfect level much easier. Knowing about story structure can't guarantee you'll get it right every time, but it can help you figure out when you've got it wrong, and that goes a long, long way.

Finally, at the very end of the third act, we have the denouement, also know as the resolution. In Star Wars, this would be the medal ceremony at the very end were we all cheer for our heroes. Such a thing might seem like pointless fan-pleasing fluff, but the resolution is actually one of the most important parts of the book.

When you come down off something as exciting as a climax, you need time to enjoy your victory. Imagine a book where the final villain died and that was the end. No wrap-up, no celebration, just *THE END*. It would feel truncated, cut off. As a reader, you would feel angry, cheated. Where's the celebration? Where's the *ending*? This rage is universal. Even though the story technically ends with the destruction of the Death Star, everyone wants to know how our heroes ended up, even if it's just a single line. Audiences want closure, if you don't give it to them, if you try to cheat them on the resolution, it doesn't matter how well you pulled off everything else. They will hate you forever.

This doesn't mean you have to end your book happily. A denouement can be filled with grieving or bitter regrets, so long as we get to see it. The point of the denouement isn't happiness or sadness or even wrapping things up neatly. The point is tension relief. The tension of the climax must be released for a reader to feel satisfied that the book has, in fact, ended. If you as the author do not give them that satisfaction, people are going to feel swindled no matter how grand your climax was, and the last thing you want is for your reader to close your book feeling cheated and grumpy. So if you want good reviews and future sales, don't skimp on your resolution. In some ways, it's the most important part of the enterprise.

Infinitely Nesting Acts

Once you learn to recognize the three-act structure, you'll start to see it everywhere, and not just in books. The pattern shows up in all sorts of weird places, from marketing to video games—even in the election cycle. And more interesting still, it's infinitely nesting. The same structure of rising action, climax, and release can be also used on a chapter level, or a paragraph level. Books in a series can each have a three-act structure individually while being part of the larger three-act structure of the overarching meta-plot.

For example: in my Eli Monpress series, book one, *The Spirit Thief*, follows the classic three-act structure almost too rigidly (what? it was my second novel ever), but it could also be seen as the first act of the larger series. The next three books—*The Spirit Rebellion*, *The Spirit Eater*, and *The Spirit War*—all follow the three-act structure individually, but at the same time, they are part of the rising action of the series as a whole. Act II, if you will. The third act of the series kicks off at the end of *The Spirit War* in a cliff-hanger than has gotten me a lot of angry mail from fans over having to wait months for the final book, *Spirit's End*, which acts as the third act, climax, and conclusion of the series.

That said, *Spirit's End* itself is not all climax. Even though it's the big finale for my series, it's still a book in its own right, and it follows a three-act structure of its own (though, granted, one with a much larger third act than my other novels). Still, I'd like to point out that, of my five-book series, I had one book for Act I, three books for Act II, and one book for Act III. This is a pretty even spread, if I do say so myself. Most of the events in the series are rising action, with the setup and climax being the smaller thirds. Perfect traditional three-act structure and a solid, time tested way to a build fun, readable series that has a definite beginning, middle, and end.

So What Does This Have to Do with Writing Fast Again?

Everything. Remember, the core part of the writing triangle is knowledge. In day-to-day terms, this means knowing what you're going to write before you write it, but in the bigger picture of your life as a writer, it means understanding your story choices on a deeper level. If you want your writing process to be fast and reliable, it's not enough to just trust your feelings for what works. You need to know *why* it works and *how* it works if you ever want to make it work for you.

Just as an architect who understands the physics of steel and glass on a fundamental level can design beautiful, ground-breaking, but structurally sound buildings on a regular basis, so can an author who understands how stories work write high quality novels at the pace needed to make a living in publishing. The three-act structure is a tool that can help you see and understand patterns in your work, but it's hardly the only one. The truth is you can and probably will spend your entire writing life learning how stories work, but that's okay. Constantly learning new ways to be better is part of the enjoyment of mastering a skill. The best writers are the ones who are willing to think critically about what they're really doing when they sit down to write a novel. Otherwise, you're just writing blind.

That said, understanding structures even on a deep level doesn't mean ignoring your instincts. I've made several big story decisions mostly because they just felt right to me. This is because my subconscious reader mind often understands story better than my conscious writer brain, which sometimes can't see the forest for the trees.

But trusting your gut is different from being at its mercy. The more I write and look critically at my writing, the deeper my knowledge becomes, and the better I get. I spot flaws faster, which means I spend less time in rewrites. I plot better, I figure out which ideas are good and which are duds more quickly. Edits move faster because I can now spot where I went wrong on a structural level. I won't say writing gets easier, because I don't think it ever does, but my ability to handle it quickly, competently, and professionally has grown exponentially since I started making a serious effort to understand how writing works. I'm still learning—hopefully, I always will be—but I get faster and better every day, and that is an incredible feeling.

The Two Bird Minimum

Now that we've talked about setup and characters and structure, it's time to move on to the actual writing part of things. Namely, I'd like to address those problematic building blocks of every story: scenes.

In my Eli Monpress series, Eli, my charming degenerate of a main character, has a favorite saying: "My stones have a two-bird minimum." Naturally, since these are my books and Eli is my character, this is also one of *my* favorite sayings, and I try to apply it as often as possible. Especially in my writing, and *especially* when I'm planning out a scene.

First, through, a little terminology.

The Three Hooks

If you ask twenty authors what makes a scene, you'll probably get twenty different answers. Some people insist scenes must take place within the same time or place, others claim a scene is just an arbitrary division used to organize action within a story. Personally, I've written all sorts of scenes, including ones that traveled through galaxies and ones that spanned years. I've had scenes that didn't have characters in them and scenes that were nothing but dialog. So yeah, lots and lots of different ways to write, define, and think about scenes. So many, in fact, that defining one set of rules for scenes is itself problematic. With that in mind, rather than trying to fit my scenes into rules no one can agree on, I prefer to set goals. Specifically, I ask that my scenes do three things:

- Advance the story
- Reveal new information
- Pull the reader forward

That's it. That's the quota a scene must achieve to stay in Rachel's story. I don't care how the scene does it. It can be one sentence long, but so long as it hits all three of these points, we're good.

Speaking of one-sentence scenes puts me in mind of a great example I got from one of fantasy author Holly Lisle's writing articles. She was actually talking about what makes a chapter (which is a lot like what makes a scene, only with the added bonus that something has to change), and to illustrate her point, she used a chapter from one of Lawrence Block's Chip Harrison novels. This example chapter, which came at the midpoint of the book in question, consisted of only one line: "Chip, I'm pregnant."

And *that* is why I avoid tying down scenes with rules. There's no rule in any writing book that would allow a chapter like that, and yet it works so beautifully. In those three words, the story advanced, new information was revealed, the reader was pulled forward, and the entire plot—the main character's entire *life*—changed. Also, by doing it in one sentence, the author created a hell of a sucker punch and a guaranteed page turn from his readers.

So that's an extreme example of a scene. Realistically of course, your scenes are going to be a lot bigger than one sentence. Mine have run anywhere from 200 words to the mid-3000s depending on how much needed to be done. Note that phrase, "needed to be done," because that's what scenes do in a novel. They get things done.

Each scene is a step toward the end of your story. Every time you have a scene, you move the novel forward until, scene by scene, you reach the end.

By that same logic, though, you have to take care to place your steps wisely. As I've mentioned before, prime publishable length for a traditionally published novel is usually considered to be between 80k and 100k words (120k for fantasy). That means, if you assume an average scene length of 2000 - 2500 words, you've only got 40-50 steps before you're out of room.

Forty steps might sound like a lot, but when you're dealing with a complicated plot and multiple characters, it can shrink amazingly. And as someone with, *ahem*, word count problems (*Spirit's End* topped out at 170,000), this is an area of writing I spend a *lot* of time worrying about. When I started my new series (the one that began with my twelve-day novel, for those of you keeping score at home), I knew right from the start that I would have to learn to tell my stories in fewer words. Part of this could be achieved through tighter wordcraft, but there's only so much you can cut out of your sentences before they become unreadable. If I was going to make a real difference in my word count without sacrificing story or complexity, I needed a more systematic solution.

Better, Faster, Stronger

Fortunately, the secret turned out to be obvious. The only way to get actually shorter novels is to have *fewer scenes.* Simple, right? Well, no, because while I needed shorter books, I wasn't about to start sacrificing plot. So, the question became how to have fewer scenes without having to cut story? The answer: make each scene do more.

By this point, I'd been using my three scene requirements—advance the story, reveal new information, and pull the reader forward—for a long time. Now, though, I started asking "What else can this scene do?" I forced myself to really look at what was going on in a scene and ask, "Where else can I put plot?" Sure the three hook quota had been met for one story line, but could I squeeze in others? Sometimes the answer was no, but just by asking the question I started seeing new ways in which my story lines could twist together.

For example, say you have a scene that is vital to the main story line, like the point where your main character first discovers the truth of her magic. There is absolutely no way this scene can be cut, but that doesn't mean it can't pick up some extra work. For example, say you also have a romantic subplot going where the love interest has secretly been ordered to keep our heroine from learning what she really is. You could have a separate scene afterward where he tries to convince her what she's just discovered is bunk, or a scene before where he tries to prevent her from discovering it in the first place... *or* you could combine the two scenes together.

Once we smash the scenes together, we end up with our heroine discovering the truth of her magic while the hero tries to hold her back, which is some super tension. We're advancing the story, revealing new information, and pulling the reader forward on both of these plot lines at once, *and* we've created a crisis moment that will keep the reader turning pages. We've made a tighter, leaner, better story, all by combining two scenes into one.

You can't do this with every scene, of course. Sometimes you need to keep your focus tight on one story line; other times it just doesn't work out logistically. That said, some of my best scenes and most dramatic scenes have actually been the ones I've combined to get my word count down. True, doubling up can be a pain in the tuckus, but for my money, combining scenes is always preferable to cutting them. And even if you're not having word count problems, just asking "What else can I do here?" every time you look at a scene will keep your mind open to myriad, often wonderful, possibilities.

The Tyranny of Word Count

I am not unaware of the irony of talking about tactics to create shorter novels in a book whose premise is all about upping word count. But while I do adore making my word count go up in large jumps—I can't help it! I love making numbers bigger. It's why I played World of Warcraft!—no writer will ever claim that writing is about the number of words. In fact, fatter novels are much harder to sell than slimmer ones, and flabby novels don't sell at all. So even though I hope with all my might that my methods help you write more words every day, if all we're adding is bulk and not substance, we're doing more harm than good.

My ultimate goal as a writer is to be able to put out fantastic novels as efficiently as possible. I think that fast writing, especially at the first draft stage, is fun, inspiring, and freeing. But fast as I go, I never lose sight of the real purpose: to tell a good story. I don't think I have to say that quality of words trumps quantity every single time, because if you've ever read a good book, you already know that. So don't be afraid to slow down and be inefficient if that's what you need to do. It's your book and your story. Enjoy it, and never be afraid to do whatever it takes to make your novel as good as it possibly can be.

Editing for People Who Hate Editing

Now that we've plotted our novel and (hopefully) written it at double time with only a few minor false trails, it's time to enter the dark and terrifying forest that lurks at the end of all writing journeys. I'm talking, of course, about editing.

Other than whether or not *The Spirit War* will be available on audio book (for the *last time*, they haven't bought the rights, so I have no idea. I'm sorry), the vast majority of questions I get in my e-mail concern editing in some way. I can totally understand why so many people want help. Editing can be very intimidating, especially if you've never done it before—or worse, tried to edit and quit in frustration.

Personally, I used to dread edit time like a cat dreads a bath. It was the point in the process when I actually had to confront all the big, scary problems I'd been putting off during the first draft. And then there was the part where, by the time I'd read my book the requisite million times it took me to finish an edit to my satisfaction, I invariably hated my story, my characters, my writing, and often myself. Not fun times.

But with thirteen finished books under my belt, I've come around to a different way of thinking. These days, editing is probably my favorite part of the writing process. This is largely because my new plotting steps let me spot and fix most horrible problems at the beginning when they're easy as opposed to during editing when they are suicide-inducing (this would be the gallon of blood that pint of sweat saved), but it's also because I've recently started thinking about editing in a whole new light. A new light that I'm now going to attempt to explain in the hopes that others can avoid the years I spent banging my head against things.

But Rachel, I HATE Editing!

I hear this all the time in a million different variations. Hell, I used to say this myself. Now, though, when someone tells me they hate editing, I say: No, you don't.

Editing is writing. If you like writing, you like editing. Editing is just the part of writing that comes at the end when you're weary and things are hardest, which earns it a lot of bad press. However, what most people fail to realize is that editing, like writing, is a *skill*. Like any skilled activity, it gets better and easier with practice and attention. Just as each pie baked makes you a better baker, each house designed makes you a better architect, and each book written makes you a better writer, so does each editorial process make you a better editor.

I firmly believe that every good writer can become a good editor if they're not one already. The same skills that make you a good storyteller make you a good story perfecter, you just have to stop hating the process and start treating your editing like you treat your writing – something you strive to be good at, something you do every day, and something that you want to make a career out of. Because trust me, if you're a pro writer, you're going to spend a large part of your career editing. A writer who ignores her or her editing skill is like a carpenter who can design and build a table but completely dismisses sanding and finishing. Sure it's a working table, maybe even a really nice table, but no one's going to want to sit at it and get splinters in their elbows.

Okay, Ms. Smarty-Pants, How Do I Get Better at Editing?

The most effective way is to write a lot of books and edit them, though I admit that's not the most practical solution, especially for people who are trying to get their first book ready for sale. Another good way to learn about editing is to edit other people's work, but this can be chancy since it's hard to bridge the gap between finding someone else's problems and learning to see and solve your own. So, if you're in a hurry to learn how to edit your own work quickly and effectively, here's how I do it.

Step 1: Change the Way You Think about Editing

What is editing, specifically? When you're editing a novel, what are you actually doing? Sure, you're revising the prose to make it prettier and you're fixing character issues and patching plot holes and so on, but what are you *really* doing? What is the point of all this work? Even getting the novel ready to go to a publisher is still only a step, not the end goal. So what is the final destination of editing?

Answer: Reader experience.

When you write a first draft, you are writing a story. You're telling your character's tale, spinning your adventure, whatever. When you start to edit a novel, though, you're no longer just telling what happened. You're getting ready to put on a production, to invite a reader into your world. Think of your book as an amusement park fun house. You might have built it based on your fantasies, but once you invite people inside, it's no longer yours alone. The world you've created now has to make sense to others. It has to delight and surprise and, most importantly, capture them. Readers can be drawn in by the glitz at the front door, but from the moment they set foot inside your domain, it's your job to keep them there.

This, for me, is what editing is about. You are no longer just getting words down, no longer asking "What happens next?" You're asking "How can I prepare the reader for what happens next?" and "How can I make them *love* it?"

You're not just writing a story anymore. You are crafting an experience that you are going to share with each person who picks up your book. It is *your job* to make sure your story decisions and world work not just within the context of the novel, but within the mind of the reader. Your job to make sure your characters are engrossing, not just effective for moving your plot forward. Your job to give these people a reason to stay.

I hold out my hand to the reader and say, "Let me show you something amazing." The reader grabs hold and off we run down the path to worlds that don't exist until I imagined them. Editing is the process of perfecting that path. I *told* you it was awesome.

Step 2: Editing Tools

Overblown rhetoric aside, let's get down to the nuts and bolts of the business. When I finish a book, I usually give it one night before I jump into editing. Some people like to wait and give the story time to settle, but I'm impatient and prefer to strike while my understanding of the book is still fresh. This is a personal choice, though, so do whatever feels right for you.

The first thing I do in any edit is identify what's wrong with the book. The reasoning behind this is the same I used to up my word count: knowledge makes you go faster. Just as you write more words per hour when you know what you're writing about, you solve problems faster when you know what those problems are. Simple, right?

Well, sort of. Identifying what needs fixing in a story is actually a lot more complicated than it seems like it should be. Some problems are obvious right off the bat; others are more subtle and might not come out until you really dig into the edit. These are the problems I have to hunt, and for that, I use three tools: a scene map, a time line, and a to-do list.

The Scene Map

If you've read the chapter about how I plot novels, you'll recognize this. A scene map is just a very quick jot down of what happens in the book broken up by scene and chapter, exactly like the scene list I made back at the plotting stage of things. Of course, you'll want to make a new list to reflect what you actually wrote instead of what you planned since there's almost certainly been some drift, but the general idea is the same. For example, here's an entry from the scene map I made for the book I just finished editing:

Ch 1 (7452)
- D gets Caldswell tip from Anthony
- D goes to starport, checks the tip, sees the Fool
- D has her interview, impressive, gets the

job

Very simple, very short hand, you're not writing a synopsis here. The point of the scene map is to be a guide, a literal scene-by-scene map of what happens in your book.

Why do I do this? Well, when I finish a novel, there may be scenes back at the beginning I haven't looked at in weeks, possibly months. A scene map helps refresh my memory, while at the same time helping me see the overall flow of my novel laid out in simple list form.

Also, with a scene map, identifying plot lines becomes very easy. I often print my map out and highlight the scenes in different color markers to denote what plot lines they touch—love story scenes, main plot scenes, secondary plot scenes, etc. This lets me see how my book is put together in a new and cheerfully colored way that can clearly illustrate problems that might otherwise be hard to pin down. For example, if I have a giant block of one color at the beginning but nowhere else, that's a clear sign that my story is uneven, and I should probably fix that.

This kind of arts and crafts approach might not sound like your thing, but I highly suggest you try it at least once. I think you'll be surprised by how useful it can be.

(**Silly but useful tip:** Notice that number in parenthesis beside the chapter marker in the example? That is how I note the chapter's word count. I do this with every chapter in my scene map as a way of making sure sure all my chapters are roughly the same length. Since I have Scrivener—which already lays this info out for me on the manuscript page—I don't really need to do this, but if you're not using Scrivener, I totally recommend marking each chapter's word count somewhere you can compare them so you can spot any anomalies. For example, if you have one 4k chapter and one 8k chapter right next to each other, the 8k will feel like it's dragging no matter how good the tension is. It's always good to keep an eye on these things.)

Finally, a scene map lets me easily jump around from scene to scene inside my book, a benefit that will become apparent very shortly.

The Time Line

Again, this is just like the one I did back during the plotting phase, only now I redo it to reflect what was actually written. Since I just went through the novel to make my scene map, I use that to make a quick time line of all the relevant events that happen in the novel. Once I've got those down, I go back again and write in what all my characters were doing when they weren't present for an event, especially if they were doing something else important "off screen."

I usually draw my time lines by hand in my notebook, and I never draw them to scale. This time line's value as a tool is less about showing the relative distance between events and more about keeping track of what happens in what order, who's together at what times, and where everyone is when important events occur. So really it's more like a time and space line, but you get the idea. (Of course, this is just my preference since I'm really bad at drawing to-scale time lines. If creating massive, detailed charts of your story's events sounds like fun to you, go for it!)

If a scene map is a visual guide to your book, a time line is a fault-finding device for your plot. Just drawing it out can reveal information flow problems you never considered before, like if a villain knows the heroes are coming before they decide to go, that kind of thing. It can also help point out places where the action is too loose or too tight (if you have a huge cluster of events taking place in one hour, for example), identify where tension might be lagging (these tend to be big blank spots), and show when a character's been out of the picture for too long. My villains especially seem to spend a lot of time sitting around doing nothing, which is dumb. Characters with enough motivation to be antagonists do not sit on their hands! A time line helps me see and fix this problem.

It doesn't have to be the best drawn time line in the world, but I do suggest putting in the effort to make it usable. You might be the only one who will be looking at the thing, but do you really want to use a crappy tool? Of course not. Take the time to do it right, and you'll find your time line has all kinds of unexpected uses.

The To-Do List

So now that you've built your scene map and

your time line, it's time to start putting your novel through the wringer to squish out the problems. Back at the top of this step, I mentioned that some problems are obvious right from the beginning. These are the ones that go at the top of your to-do list. Also, you might have found some more problems while you were making your time line and scene maps, so go ahead and put these down as well.

At this point, you're basically making a giant pile of things that need to be addressed. I like to type mine into a table in Google Drive so I can color-code things and move them around (I'm anal that way), but you can use whatever you want: a note pad, napkins, index cards, etc. Anything with a lot of room for new entries that's easy to access and won't get lost will do, but keep it close at hand, because you're going to be adding to it a lot.

Once I've written out every problem with my book I've found so far, I organize them on my to-do list by how hard they'll be to fix, starting with the largest and most complicated and ending with the smallest. See, editing is like cleaning a house. You know how you don't vacuum before you dust because otherwise the dust will get all over your nicely vacuumed floor? Editing is the same. Solving problems is a messy business, and you don't want that mess getting all over scenes you've already edited. So rather than work linearly through a book from beginning to end, I work on each problem separately starting with the biggest and making my way down. (More on this in the next step.)

Step 3: Actually Editing

Making my tools and getting my to-do list organized usually takes me about a day, two if the book is really complicated and/or messed up. Once the chores are done, though, it's time to get down to brass tacks.

Fixing the big stuff

As I mentioned up in the to-do list, I edit from biggest problem to smallest, not from first page to last. I know this feels counter intuitive. After all, you wrote the book from beginning to end, so page one seems like the natural place to start editing. However, I maintain that the beginning of your book is actually the *worst* place to start, and here's why.

Say you're getting ready to begin your edit. You've got a to-do list full of problems to be solved, so you click over to the very beginning of your manuscript to get to work. Ah, but all those problems you listed don't happen in order, do they? And they don't all happen at once, either. Let's say the first problem on your list is fixing your main character's motivation. Chances are, that motivation pops up all over the book. Maybe you see it at the very beginning, a few times in the middle, and then again at the big climax. But in between those problem scenes is the rest of your story, so what do you do?

Well, if you started your edit at the beginning, you would now have two choices. You could try to hold the entire to-do list in your head as you worked, fixing each problem as it appears, but this quickly gets unwieldy, especially if you're dealing with multiple large, thorny problems. Also, it's slow. If you're editing from front to back, there could be weeks between when you fix the first part of a problem in chapter one and the last part of a problem in chapter twenty. Unless you're a human supercomputer or you keep fantastic notes, chances are you'll have forgotten some of what you were trying to-do in the intervening time, leaving you scrambling back to reread what you did before you move on.

So clearly this method isn't ideal, but if you want to stick to your narrative, the only other option is to do multiple passes through the text, one for each major problem. This would keep you focused, but if you're not already cringing at the idea of reading your book that many times, you have a stronger disposition than I do.

The real issue here isn't that working from "Once Upon a Time" to "The End" is fundamentally flawed, but that problems in books tend to be non-linear. Some are localized to specific chapters (like flagging tension in a battle scene). Others are as pervasive as poison ivy, rearing their ugly heads in varying degrees all through the narrative. Each of these issues deserves your full attention, but if you're chained to the linear narrative, your book is actually getting in your way. You've got all this text between you and the different parts of the problem you're attempting to solve.

So how do you edit quickly and effectively? Easy. You jump.

Using my scene map and time line, I can move through my novel in a completely non-linear fashion without getting lost. This means I can pick one problem to solve and then jump to every place where it occurs. This way, I'm treating each instance as part of a cohesive whole, a single narrative line, rather than islands separated by thousands of words. And because I'm only solving one problem at a time rather than trying to keep an entire novel in my head, I can usually set thing right in short order, allowing me to cross the item off my to-do list and move on. This ability to jump in, fix the problem everywhere it appears, and then keep going isn't just efficient. It also creates an invaluable sense of progress and motion that is directly opposed to the usual nightmarish, running-in-place lethargy that editing can evoke.

Working this way after years of front-to-back editing did take some adjustment. Now that I've got the hang of it, though, I'm never going back. Doing a linear, start-to-finish revision while keeping everything I needed to change later in my head felt like trying to juggle a hundred balls at once. The whole process seemed eternally on the verge of disaster, and as I got more and more stressed, my book's problems looked more and more unfixable until failure seemed inevitable. This was not a healthy, fun, or effective way to work. It took forever, it made me miserable, and I often had to edit a book several times to actually get it right.

Now, though, by using my tools to move freely through the text and keeping a to-do list that not only helps me keep track of what needs to be done, but lets me look and see how much further I have to go, I keep control. The edit no longer rules me, it's no longer overwhelming or stressful, and best of all, I don't hate my book at the end. I'm free to enjoy the editing process, and as a result, I've gotten a lot better at it. I now edit faster, better, and with far less pain than ever before. Writing 10k words a day might sound a lot more impressive than efficient editing, but this is actually the change that has made the biggest difference in my writing life.

The Read-Through

So far I've been focusing on fixing the big problems, the book breakers, but once every item on my to-do list has been crossed off, it's time to move into the read through. By this point in the process, I've usually visited every scene in my novel at least twice, and though the big issues have all been addressed, my efficient non-linear editing process has left bits of uncorrected text all over. It's not uncommon for me to have mentions of characters who no longer exist or references to events that no longer happen lying about all over. If editing is like renovating a house, then all the structural work is done, but there's drywall dust and nails all over the floor and the walls all need to be painted. In short, my book is a MESS, and it's time for a serious cleanup.

This is the read-through's job. *Now* I go back to page one and start reading, putting things in order as I go. This is my line edit, the part of the process where I clean up all the out-of-place bits. This is also where I try to really finesse the book. I examine word choice, polish my hooks to a shine, and fiddle with chapter endings until everything is just how I want it. Fortunately, since I've already addressed all my big problems, I am free to do this sort of high touch work without worrying about if I'm just going to have to change it all later. The big problems are already conquered, the hard part is over, and I'm now clear to sweat the small stuff as much as I want. It's very liberating.

Sometimes in my read-through, though, I'll find a few more items for my to-do list. If the problems are small, I just go ahead and fix them on the spot, but I save any big stuff I find until the end. When my read-through is done, I go back and address anything that still needs fixing until my to-do list is completely scratched out again. Then, if necessary, I'll do one more pass over any chapters I might have messed up during the last fixes. Once this is done, I'm almost ready to declare my novel officially edited. There's only one thing left to do.

Step 4: Activating the Reader Brain

My book is now about as good as I can make it. Oh sure, there are still things I can tweak (there are *always* things I can tweak), but generally speaking, I'm pretty happy with the whole affair. However, I don't send the manuscript off just yet. First, I need to make sure I'm not deluding myself about the book being good. It's time for the final test. If I'm going be sure I'm really seeing the forest instead of the trees, I have to back away and read my book like a reader instead of a writer.

This is a pretty hard trick to pull off, especially for a book you've just finished working on. Lots of authors like to put their novel in a drawer for a few months and get distance that way, but as I said, I'm impatient. I want that book done *now*. So, to make this final hurdle, I had to find a way to trick my brain into thinking like a reader.

I did it by using my Kindle.

Since I do almost all my pleasure reading on my Kindle and all my writing on my laptop, putting my book onto my Kindle allows me to disconnect from the writer side of my brain and actually get into my novel as a story instead of a project. Also, since I can't edit the text at all while it's on the Kindle, I'm forced to relax and just enjoy the book. I keep a notebook handy in case I do find things, of course, but mostly I just read, which can be a pretty intense thing all by itself. Let me tell you, there is no better feeling in the world than reading something you wrote and thinking "Wow, this is actually pretty good!"

And That's a Wrap!

If I can read through my entire book on my Kindle without any huge red flags popping up, the edit is officially done. It's now time to send the novel on to its next stage of existence. For me, that means giving it to my husband/beta reader to see if it's ready to go to my agent.

(You'll notice how I didn't mention beta readers before this, right? Well, that's because I don't believe in using beta readers before I've edited my book completely myself. First, I think its rude to ask someone to read something as unfinished as a typical first draft, and second, if I rely on others to spot my problems for me, then I'm not growing as an editor or a writer. Save the fresh, foreign eyeballs for the problems you can't find on your own. Anything else is a waste of everyone's time.)

My husband will usually find a few issues I missed, so I'll go back and make corrections and maybe take a last look at any problem areas. Then, when I feel confident, I send the manuscript off to my editor and/or agent, depending on if this book is already sold or not. If you're still in the process of finding an agent, this is where you'd write a query letter. If you're self-publishing, this is where you'd send it off to your hired editor. Whatever your manuscript's final destination, though, don't let it go anywhere before you let someone you trust to be honest and thorough have a look at it. The Internet has lots of excellent established writing groups that can help you with this if you don't have the good fortune of having an amazing beta reader chained to you by matrimony.

The Wheel of Edits Turns...

Of course, no matter how carefully I edit a book, it will still come back from my editor full of notes. This is as it should be. If I could catch everything myself, we wouldn't need editors! Every time notes come back, I do my editorial process over again. I update my scene map and time line, make a to-do list, organize the problems, etc.

My books usually go through three rounds of edits before they enter official production, but it's very personal. How many edits you need with depend on your your book.

A Note for the First-Time Novelist

With all the pressure on first-time novelists these days to produce a flawless draft, it can be tempting to edit your book over and over in a quest for perfection. Once, I met a writer who'd edited her first novel over thirty times! It's not that I don't understand the impulse—there are still things in *The Spirit Thief* that I wish I could go back and change—but there is such a thing as editing too much.

Every edit you do has diminishing returns. The

first few are vital, but after a certain point you're just moving words around and wasting your time. Sooner or later, you have to say good-bye and turn that sucker in.

So if you don't have a publishing deadline yet, set one for yourself. Don't let your editing become an endless process. You've got a lot of books to write, after all. Never one novel monopolize your time and keep you from writing all that you can write!

Bonus! Tips for a Happy, Low-Stress Edit

Every edit is as different as the book it's trying to fix. Some novels come out almost perfect; others... less so. Planning at the beginning helps you avoid the worst problems, but it's impossible to anticipate everything. Even with a non-linear edit and good tools, the editing process is still one of faultfinding and self-examination, and that can be harrowing. So, here are a few general tips I've found that help me keep my cool through the final stage of my novel.

#1 - Don't be too hard on yourself

I said at the very beginning that editing is a skill, and I've found that I'm a lot happier if I treat it as such. Editing is hard, especially if you haven't done it much yet. You wouldn't get mad at someone who couldn't play the piano perfectly after their very first lesson, would you? Of course not, so don't hate on yourself if your first edit goes less than smoothly. Don't get frustrated when you don't know how to solve a problem. Instead, step back and think of things in the bigger picture.

Most importantly, edit daily. Just like you write every day during the first draft, during the editing process, edit every day. If you get stuck, move on to another problem, but always remember that you are *practicing a skill*, and unless you're a savant, you're not going to be fantastic at the start. Have patience with yourself and your book. If you learned enough about writing to reach "The End," you can learn enough about editing to get your manuscript ready for publication. Don't give up!

#2 - Trust your instincts

I've talked about gut reactions before, but they're especially important here. If you care enough about stories to want to write them, you probably have good storytelling instincts. Maybe you can't explain it, but you like some scenes better than others. Conversely, you might hate a scene and not know why. With the lack of any easily identifiable problem, it can be tempting to just ignore the nagging feeling and move on. Don't. You got your instincts over years of exposure to the best stories our world can deliver, books and movies and plays that have survived not only commercial production, but also the test of time. Trust your gut. If you dislike a scene, that means something is wrong. Go back and figure out what it is. Never put a scene you don't love in your book.

#3 – No problem is unfixable

There is no slog like a bad edit, and when you're first learning how to fix a book, there's no avoiding a bad time. I have never, ever been as depressed about writing as I got during the edits for *The Spirit Rebellion*—my second Eli novel and the very first book I wrote under contract. I'm generally a pretty happy person, but there were days I just didn't want to get out of bed because I couldn't stand to deal with stupid head-against-brick-wall problems any longer.

But no problem is truly unfixable. When you're writing a book, you are god. You can change anything, which means there is no corner you can paint yourself into that you cannot get out of. True, finding a solution that works might be difficult, and you might not get the right solution on the first try, but it *will* come. You might need to cut off someone's arm to get there, but you will always reach "The End" if you are willing to open your mind, embrace your limited divinity, and think beyond the plot.

"What Advice Do You Have for New Writers?"

As a professional writer who also writes about writing, I do a lot of interviews. My Q&A sessions range from the silly to the serious, but the one question that always comes up without fail is, "What advice do you have for new writers?"

I used to respond to this with the same old mantra: write every day, don't give up, believe in yourself, etc. Now, there's nothing wrong with this, *per se*. It's good advice, necessary to success, but it's also the *exact same thing* everyone who's ever picked up a pen will tell you about writing. So, in the spirit of expanding the dialogue and to address an issue that I feel far more passionately about, I've decided to change my answer.

See, I have a bad habit of lurking on writing message boards, especially around November, when the NaNoWriMo (National Novel Writing Month) excitement sets in. I like being around so much energy and creativity, especially when I'm feeling down about my own work. Also, every now and then I find these amazing gems... and I will leave the definition of 'gem' in that sentence to your imagination. But sometimes (okay, most of the time), reading these boards makes me angry, especially the forums where people talk about publication. Specifically, I lose my cool when people start commenting on whether or not something is "allowed."

It usually starts innocently. A new writer will put up a post asking whether or not it's okay to combine subgenres (eg, an epic fantasy with superhero elements or a steampunk vampire romance (*Note to Self: write steampunk vampire romance*)), or if editors will automatically reject a werewolf book, or if you're allowed to put horror elements in your Regency—you get the idea.

These innocent questions often wind up spurring debates over the various pros and cons of this or that kind of book and what is or isn't good to write. As the thread goes on, you'll get all sorts of people—most of whom with no publishing background or access to sales numbers—saying "Oh, well, you can't write *that*" or "That won't sell" for pages and pages. Or, I assume they go on for pages. I can't say for sure, because usually by the time I reach the end of the first page my husband is trying to pry the keyboard out of my hands before I post something I'll regret.

So, to answer the question of "What advice do you have for new writers?" once and for all (and to keep myself from turning into the worst kind of enraged forum troll), I would like to say:

THERE ARE NO WRITING POLICE

If you are a writer, and you have a novel idea that you are excited about writing, write it. Don't go on message boards and ask random Internet denizens whether or not something is allowed.

Or, if you're a feedback junkie and you just *can't* keep yourself from posting, do NOT go pulling things *you* like out of *your* novel because some forum person told you your idea "won't sell."

Who is the writer here? YOU ARE. Whose book is it? YOUR BOOK. There are no writing police. No one is going to arrest you if you write a teen vampire novel post *Twilight*. No one is going to send you off to a desert island to live a wretched life of worm eating and regret because your book includes things that could be seen as cliché.

If you have a book that you want to write, just write the damn thing. Don't worry about selling it; that comes later. Instead, worry about making your book good. Worry about the best way to order your scenes to create maximum tension, worry about if your character's actions are actually in character; worry about your grammar. DON'T worry about which of your stylistic choices some potential future editor will use to reject you, and for the love of My Little Ponies don't worry about trends. Trying to catching a trend is like trying to catch a falling knife—dangerous, foolhardy, and often ending in tears, usually yours.

I'm not saying you shouldn't pay attention to what's getting published; keeping an eye on what's going on in your market is part of being a smart and savvy writer. But remember that every you book you see hitting the shelves today was sold over a year ago, maybe two.

Even if you do hit a trend, there's no guarantee the world won't be totally different by the time that book comes out. The only certainty you have is your own enthusiasm and love for your work, which is why you should never sacrifice an element that makes your novel exciting to *you* just because someone else already used it, and you should never ever *ever* take something you love about your book out because you think it will hurt your sales, *especially* if you haven't even finished the novel yet and all sales are as yet hypothetical.

Until your novel starts racking up actual rejections from people whose job it is to know what sells in publishing (or, in the case of self publishing, you're not selling at all), never change anything unless you're doing it to make the book better. If your YA urban fantasy features fairies, vampires, and selkies and you decide halfway through that the vampires are over-complicating the plot, that is an appropriate time to ax the bloodsuckers. If you decide to cut them because you're worried there are too many vampire books out right now, then you are betraying yourself, your dreams, and your art.

If you're like pretty much every other author in

the world, you became a writer because you had stories you wanted to tell. Those are your stories, and no one can tell them better than you can. So write your stories, and then edit your stories until you have something you can be proud of. Write the stories that excite you, stories you can't wait to share with the world because they're just so amazing. If you want to write *Murder She Wrote* in space with anime-style mecha driven by cats, *go for it*. Nothing is off limits unless you do it badly.

And if you must obsess over something, obsess over stuff like tension and pacing and creating believable characters. You know, the shit that matters. There are no writing police. This is *your* story, no one else's. Tell it like you want to.

And Then We Came to the End

And with that rant about Internet forums out of the way, we have come to the end of the book! I hope you enjoyed the journey and, more importantly, that you found something in my methods that will work for you as well as it's worked for me.

If you found the information in this book useful, or even if you didn't, I hope you'll consider leaving a review. Reviews, good and bad, are vital to any author's career, and I would be extremely appreciative if you'd consider writing one for me.

If you want to know more about my fiction, you can all my books at **www.rachelaaron.net**. That's also where you'll find my writing blog, *Pretentious Title*, where the original 2k to 10k post debuted and where I still talk about writing, plot, and craft. I hope you'll swing by and say hello.

Until then, thank you for reading. Now go write something!

Happy writing!
Rachel Aaron

Want more books by Rachel Aaron? Check out these titles!

HEARTSTRIKERS
Nice Dragons Finish Last
One Good Dragon Deserves Another
No Good Dragon Goes Unpunished
A Dragon of a Different Color
Last Dragon Standing (Coming in 2018!)

"A deliriously smart and funny beginning to a new urban fantasy series about dragons in the ruins of Detroit...inventive, uproariously clever, and completely un-put-down-able!" - **SF Signal**

"For all lovers of urban fantasy. Rachel Aaron brings her charismatic humor and superb characterization."
- **Fantasy Book Critic**

PARADOX
(written as Rachel Bach)
Fortune's Pawn
Honor's Knight
Heaven's Queen

"*Firefly*-esque in its concept of a rogue-ish spaceship family... The narrative never quite goes where you expect it to, in a good way... Devi is a badass with a heart."

- Locus Magazine

"If you liked *Star Wars*, if you like our books, and if you are waiting for *Guardians of the Galaxy* to hit the theaters, this is your book."- **Ilona Andrews**

"I JUST LOVED IT! Perfect light sci-fi. If you like space stuff that isn't that complicated but highly entertaining, I give two thumbs up!" - **Felicia Day**

THE LEGEND OF ELI MONPRESS

The Spirit Thief
The Spirit Rebellion
The Spirit Eater
The Legend of Eli Monpress (omnibus edition of the
first three books)
The Spirit War
Spirit's End

"Fast and fun, *The Spirit Thief* introduces a fascinating
new world and a complex magical system based on
cooperation with the spirits who reside in all living
objects. Aaron's characters are fully fleshed and possess
complex personalities, motivations, and backstories that
are only gradually revealed. Fans of Scott Lynch's *Lies of
Locke Lamora* (2006) will be thrilled with Eli Monpress.
Highly recommended for all fantasy readers."
- **Booklist, Starred Review**

To find out more about Rachel and read samples of all her books, visit

www.rachelaaron.net

Other places to find Rachel include:

Twitter: **@Rachel_Aaron**
Facebook: **facebook.com/RachelAaronAuthor**
Author Blog: **thisblogisaploy.blogspot.com**
Amazon: **amazon.com/author/rachelaaron**

About the Author

Rachel Aaron was born in Atlanta, GA. After a lovely, geeky childhood full of books and public television followed by an adolescence spent feeling awkward about it, she went to the University of Georgia to pursue English Literature with an eye towards getting her PhD. Upper division coursework quickly cured her of this delusion, and she graduated in 2004 with a BA and a job, which was enough to make her mother happy. She currently lives in Athens, GA with her very understanding husband, perpetual motion son, overgrown library, and fat wiener dog.

When she's not digging into the secrets of story construction, Rachel writes fun Fantasy and Urban Fantasy as **Rachel Aaron** and kick-ass Military Science Fiction with a romantic twist as **Rachel Bach**. For more about all of this, or to contact Rachel directly, visit **www.rachelaaron.net**!

Editing for the 2013 Revised Edition of 2k to 10k provided by Misti Wolanski.

Made in the USA
Las Vegas, NV
10 July 2022

51344170R00066